Praise for *Lo*

"If you pared away from religion all [obscured by sticker] fresh belief in daily miracles, if then you could situate your belief in moments of insight and wonder, and if you could make what's left as essence into poems of self-evident faith as clean and helpful as sun and rain, as rivers and familial affections, you would have this book, each page a kind of dawn. One by one, the poems in *Love Calls Us Here* gift us with something small and bright. They never say too much. Nothing fancy, nothing explained, belabored, nothing but an episode of what I have to call grace. There is no other word. Just enough." —Kim Stafford, author of *As the Sky Begins to Change*

"Chris Anderson's collection *Love Calls Us Here* gives the reader a sense of wonder and gratitude for life's joys and sorrows. For this poet, both mundane and extraordinary events are a call to meaning. From his dog eating his rosary to the death of a loved one, Anderson generously invites us in in a spirit of humility, empathy, curiosity, and openness." — Rita Simmonds, author of *Souls and the City*

"Chris Anderson's *Love Calls Us Here* evokes God's best name as Love (1 John 4:16). Not only that, throughout the entire collection one is reminded of George Herbert's understanding of prayer as 'Heaven in Ordinarie.' Take, and read." — Owen F. Cummings, Distinguished Regents' Professor of Theology, Mount Angel Seminary and author of *Deacons and the Church*

"Each poem in this lively collection drops us into the midst of things of this world—a party, a hospital room, a family at the baptismal font, a boy chasing a dog chasing a deer. In each of them we are led to a moment of awareness: God meets us here. They are deeply reassuring. They are also whimsical and poignant and surprising, sometimes breathtakingly apt. Readers will want to reread them, then hasten out and share them with friends." — Marilyn McIntyre, author of *Word by Word: A Daily Spiritual Practice*

"Tender, richly-imagined, and often wryly funny—*The scientist at the party marches up and demands / that I prove the Resurrection to him, right / there by the clam dip*—the poems in *Love Calls Us Here* bear profound and poignant witness to the sacrament of the present moment, "the only place where we experience the eternal," as Charles Simic has written. In these poems, as in Chris Anderson's previous collections, we encounter divine love alive less in the abstractions of belief than through our participation in it, in the most ordinary moments of our lives. In the title poem, a busy server abandons her trays of orders to listen to a patron's grief: *And in my mind / her kindness and the old man's grief and the mystery / of death and all the stories and the sadness / in that crowded place seem to rise up and come together [...].* In 'Valvoline,' a priest flies to a remote Alaskan village to perform Last Rites, and—having forgotten to bring his holy oil— anoints the dying man with engine lubricant. *It is hard to see the face of Jesus,* declares the speaker in "The Elements." And yet, by the light that passes through these poems, we do." —Donna Henderson, author of *The Eddy Fence*

"These poems— careful observations, graces and insights quietly shared— will awaken readers to do something of the same; that is, to notice in any given day as much as we possibly can, things large and small, and to realize we are immersed in a world of wondrous gifts, gifts delivered through loved ones and strangers, through dogs, gardens, geese, the solar system, etc. These poems are quiet celebrations and lessons for life." — Abbot Jeremy Driscoll, O.S.B., Mount Angel Abbey, author of *A Monk's Alphabet*

"These plainspoken, profound, surprising, earnest poems mark Chris Anderson as one of my favorite voices in this tangled world. Love calls us to this collection because love has called Chris Anderson to minister to the many needy people he so carefully honors—the lame, the blind, the old, the imprisoned. Those whom Jesus calls 'the least of these' are the heroes of these poems, and will become yours. Driving past a brightly lit stadium in the rural darkness, Anderson tells us, *I know that within me there / is a great love, and everywhere. / All around me. / I can't hear them but I know / that everyone is cheering*. As you read these heart-deep poems, you will soon be cheering as well." — Paul J. Willis, author of *Somewhere to Follow*

"This is the spiritual life I'd like to have—though I'm outside any tradition now, least of all his. Yet the fluid, funny, heart-broke inner life that's on display here—clever moments and deep ones alike, a spirit cheerful and enduring and kind—it's irresistible. The poems are skillful but never pat. They take unexpected turns. They are well-formed. They make me glad to be alive. Because this collection is about the life of the spirit yet resolutely nondogmatic; instead, it is attractive, human, real. Anyone can read it. Ex-baptists, ex-Catholics, practicing Catholics, regular folks with no axe to grind: all of us together around the small, perfect campfire of this book." — David Oates, author of *The Mountains of Paris*

Love Calls Us Here

Love Calls Us Here

Chris Anderson

Design by Cambridge Creative Group

Cover image: With grateful acknowledgement to Richard Thorn for permission to reproduce his painting, "Down Misty Vale."

Published by Wildhouse Poetry, an imprint of Wildhouse Publishing (www.wildhousepublishing.com).

Printed in the USA

ISBN 978-1-961741-11-9

for the boy and the girl
on Beehollow Lane

CONTENTS

II. Something Else I Didn't Understand

III. Recognition

"It is I, Beatrice...Love called me here."

– Dante, *The Inferno* II. 69 – 72

"Divine love meets us in the real world, and nowhere else:
in this moment...this person..."

– Ruth Burrows, *The Essence of Prayer*

I.

DRIVING AT NIGHT

Driving at Night

Driving at night on the way to Spokane
I see a stadium in a little town
and the lights of the stadium pouring
into the darkness.

I am passing by.

I know that within me there
is a great love, and everywhere.
All around me.

I can't hear them but I know
that everyone is cheering.

To Believe is to Remember

Someone in *Reader's Digest* said to stop
and live each moment before it slips away.

I was nine or ten, swinging on a rope
from a branch of what must have been an oak,
bumping into the trunk with my feet
and pushing off again. And I stopped,

and I dangled in the cold, wintry air,
and I looked at the bark,

wrinkly and gray like an elephant's skin,
and at the ridges in the bark,
and at the channels the ridges made.

I thought: *remember this*.

Geese

We were having Mass on a cliff above a bay.
This was after a storm, and through
the windows the rain still glistened on the alder.
And at just the moment of the consecration,
as the bread was becoming the Body of Christ,
a great flock of geese came clamoring
over us, honking and clattering.
It must have been enormous.
We could almost hear the words.

The Solar System

When I asked Mr. B about solar wind, he said
there was no such thing, in front of the whole class.
I was pretty sure he was wrong, and he was:
solar wind is a stream of charged particles, mostly

protons, released from the upper atmosphere of the sun
and permeating the Solar System. You can harness it,
like these kids in a story I'd read about a regatta
in space. Their sail unfurled for half a mile, glittering

in the blackness. But I don't blame Mr. B.
The universe is vast and mysterious,
and it's full of things we don't understand.

That year I won the Madison Elementary School
Science Fair for what I called a solar house. It was just
a plywood box, cut on the diagonal, with glass
on the slant and two thermometers, one on the inside

and one on the outside. In the morning when the sun
came up, the box got warmer and warmer,
and in the evening, when the sun set, it cooled.
Just like everything else. Like all of us.

The Trinity

She loves the Trinity.
She walks outside and looks up at the stars
and is in love with the Trinity.

She doesn't think she has enough patience
and she doesn't think she has enough love
and she doesn't. No one has.

There is another world. There is another beauty.

Every day as she drives up the hill
she passes a yellow truck rusting in a field.
It has the pleasing rounded corners.

It is so covered with vines
it has become part of the landscape.

She wonders if coyotes sleep under the chassis.
She wonders if anyone still has the keys.

Baptizing Rosa

The little girl in a gauzy white dress
and beaded tiara. The father in a pressed white shirt
and jeans, his dark face solemn and intent
as he tries to understand the words. I feel clumsy.

Distant. But then I cup the water
in my hand, and I pour it on his daughter's head,
on her jet-black hair, and I look up at him,
and he looks up at me, and for a moment we meet.

We know. The way sometimes before you fall
asleep there is an image in your mind,
or a fragrance, or a melody
you don't remember when you wake up,
the beginning of a story you only understand
at just the moment you let go.

The Scientist at the Party

The scientist at the party marches up and demands
that I prove the Resurrection to him, right
there by the clam dip. Then sniffs and walks away.
As if it it's not perfectly obvious

that the Resurrection happened. It always is.
To call consciousness an illusion is to be conscious
of an illusion. Where did the scientist come from,
for example? Not just from the living room,

and he didn't just happen to run into me at random.
He made a beeline. Nothing comes
from nothing. Imagine you're walking in a forest
and come upon a beautiful sphere glowing

in the air, big as your house. How absurd
would it be not to wonder how it got there? Now
what about the chipmunks, too, or the slugs?
The proud Douglas fir? The shy ferns?

What Happens at Mass

What happens at Mass is that a single point
explodes into a billion, billion pieces, and the pieces
fly away at incredible speeds, and they become
atoms, then gases, then stars and planets,
and on one planet amoebas appear, and the amoebas
become fish, and the fish become dinosaurs,
and the dinosaurs become monkeys and dogs, everything
is always becoming something else, until finally
the universe comes to consciousness of itself
and we're standing there looking around thinking wow,
this is really beautiful. This is really sad.

When Jesus appears in the flesh
we don't recognize him at first.
We think he's the gardener.

An old man and an old woman
walk down the breezeway with a baby.
They must be in their seventies, maybe their eighties.
The old man is bowlegged and wearing jeans.
He looks like he's worked his whole life.
The old woman has wrapped a shawl around her head
and swaddled the baby, but it's the old man
who is holding the baby as they walk.

She is four months old, they tell me.
Her name is Alice Rose.

You baptized her, the old woman says, smiling,
a couple of months ago.

The baby's head is smooth and soft
and there is a band around it, and on the band,
in the center of her forehead,
there is a little white rose made of cloth.

What happens at Mass is that I keep watching
the old man as he sits in the pew
looking down at the baby and smiling,
rocking her in his arms.

The Pilot Whale

Riding my bike to school I see a whale
that has followed a boat into the locks.
It surfaces quietly, broad back glistening,

sleek and black in the oily water.
I was crossing over on a narrow bridge.
In the distance, the spires of the city.

I was on my way to the university,
to the books and the seminars and all I was
trying to be. But now something sleek

and black has broken the surface—
a pilot whale—caught, big as a pickup,
curving and diving along the steep walls

of the lock, until the level finally drops
and it can swim away, back out
into the broad, bright waters of the sea.

Just Us

When Thomas Merton went to the church
of Cosmas and Damian, on the edge of the Forum
in Rome, and he looked up and saw
the great seventh-century mosaic, the Judgment Day,
shining above the altar, the Lord
coming in judgment in a dark blue sky,
with a suggestion of fire, he was overwhelmed.
He thought of the centuries.

I went with our little group from the parish,
and when I looked up at the Judgment Day
it seemed brand new to me.
Jesus was shiny and bright, and the disciples
were standing in a row on either side,
and there was a row of fluffy sheep below.
It was like a children's book.

One poor lamb looked so worried and wan
I thought he was about to speak.
He was half-shorn. But he seemed
friendly, too, and kind, and I was so happy
that day at Mass, with the sun
and the shepherd and the sheep.
It was just us.

Tilt-a-Whirl

I am down on all fours on a paved path
just beyond the Benton County Fairgrounds.
Who knew how dizzy a dad can get?

I have a picture of Maggie as a little girl
riding in a kiddie car. She is slowly going
around and around. She is smiling
the smile I was always afraid concealed

her disappointment. But we are older now,
and we've just been on the Tilt-a-Whirl,
and everything is spinning. *Please . . . no,*

I tell the deputy when she offers me
a ride. *Please . . . no.* As if
that long, dark path is the only way
I will ever make it home.

The Anointing

A priest goes to a village in Alaska
to anoint a dying man. Maybe he flies there
in a Cessna. But he's forgotten
the oil of the sick—he left it on the counter

in the sacristy, hundreds of miles away—
and when he asks the son for what he has
he brings him a can of Valvoline.
40-weight. But the priest goes ahead.

He anoints the man with motor oil,
forgiving his sins and getting him ready
to die, wiping off the excess
with a paper towel. It's not a problem.

All the way home he's smiling,
bumping along in the low clouds.

Waiting in the Garden

When I bake a cake, I am proud of the cake.
When someone gives me a cake, I am grateful.

My problem with eating magic mushrooms
isn't becoming one with the light
but thinking we can do it whenever we want to.

What about the rain? The labradoodle?
The man who flipped his dirt bike
only wants to walk again, and I can't promise
he ever will, however hard he prays.

Rejoice always.

I am late to see a friend
and this is what he texts me:
I am waiting in the garden.

Relinquishment

—for Robert

We retired the same year, we signed the same forms,
for the "Voluntary Relinquishment of Tenure,"
but he retired because he was dying, and that last year
I'd drive out to his farm to bring him communion.

When the word has been conveyed to you,
St. Augustine says, *does not the sound seem to say,*
the word ought to grow, and I should diminish?

It was a small farm, with a few horses and a garden.
We'd sit by the woodstove and talk about our lives
as we always had. There was a sweetness about him
and a faith, a calm, and sometimes a silence
would happen in the air of the room and I'd become
aware of the door, and the window, and the chair
in their silences, they were real, I knew they were
there, and I'd believe, too. I wouldn't be afraid.

Gradually, as the tumor grew larger in his brain,
the silences grew longer, too, until by the end
he couldn't speak at all. It was ironic.
He was a professor of speech, a lover of words—
and he had an actor's voice, rich and deep—
but I never heard any bitterness from him.

One day not long before he died, after
I'd given him the Body of Christ, as we sat there
watching the flames, he took my hand, put it
to his lips, kissed it, and put it back again.

The sound of his voice had made itself heard,
and then had gone away, Augustine says,
as though it were saying, my joy is complete.

At the Dog Show

I was sitting on a folding chair at the dog show
watching the terriers being judged when I felt a presence
behind me. I turned, and there wasn't a person
standing there, there was a dog, lying down—
a brindled mastiff, so big her head came up to my shoulder.
And she was beautiful, absolutely beautiful,
with smooth black and caramel fur. 175 pounds of her.

I'll probably snap at the nurse on my deathbed.
My mind will wander during the last rites.
But Jesus doesn't say God loves us only if we're good.
He says God so loved the world—
he says grace abounds—and when I reached out

to touch her, when I showed her my hand, she heaved
herself up, and she lumbered over,
and she put her enormous head with her enormous jowls
up against my polo shirt, and she began to probe me,
up and down, her great soft nostrils huffing
in the fabric and huffing it out, so gently, so tenderly.
I swear her head was as big as my torso.
As the whole cavity of my body.

Love Calls Us Here

We spent the day at the beach and went out to eat,
but the restaurant was crowded and they had to seat us
at the bar, and as we waited we watched the bartender,
a young woman, running back and forth trying
to keep up with her orders. And there was a man
at the bar, an old man, drinking by himself, and when
she asked as she hurried by how he was doing, he said
this was the day his wife had died, the year before,
and this was her favorite place. And I remember now
how the bartender turned, and put down her tray,
and went over and talked with that old man
for a moment, how she listened, and in my mind
her kindness and the old man's grief and the mystery
of death and all the stories and the sadness in that
crowded place seem to rise up and come together,
and it's a warm summer night, and the sun is setting
on the water, and the bright waves are coming in
and going out, darkening as they break.

Wild Iris

The boy who lived a day died years ago,
and now his mother has died.
We buried her last month.

This morning we dug a hole almost to the lid
of her coffin, then lowered the baby's coffin in.
It was sitting in the wet morning grass,
a small white box, exhumed and flown to us.
His father is shoveling back the heavy earth.

It's spring, quiet and green. In the woods,
the wild iris is blooming.

And on every purple petal there is a white
feather, and on every white feather
there is a stroke of yellow, as if someone
has quickly brushed it on.

Behind Open

When I saw the owl this morning I knew
it wasn't a great horned owl because
it didn't have the two tufts of feathers on top,
like the horns that Moses was thought
to have when he brought the tablets down.

Though this turns out to be a mistranslation
of the Hebrew, a mistake in the Vulgate
and the Douay-Rheims. Moses wasn't
horned, he was *glorified*, he was *radiant,*
as even you and I are sometimes.

When I sit at the window behind
the neon *OPEN* sign, what you might see
if you were walking down the street
is a man eating noodles who wears
the word like a blazing orange mask.

The Crown

I am sitting in a highchair in Calexico, California,
my dad bending over me with the clippers.
You can see the back of my head, shaved down
to the skin. My little boy nape.

When I got back from England my hair flowed
down to my shoulders, as long as the Lord's,
though we don't really know what he looked like.
A scruffy beard, too. A leather jacket.
I was hoping no one would know me.

See, in this one, how my hair is thinning?
I am kneeling by the stone on the Mount of Olives
where Jesus prayed the cup would pass.
Someone took it from above.
You can see all the way to the crown.

Surprised

Don't be surprised at the elevation of the host
if nothing seems to happen. The bread and wine
become the Body and Blood, but it works

the other way, too. God so loved the world
he became a metaphor. He emptied himself out.

There's that moment when you're growing older
and realize you are. There's that moment
when you look at your wife's face and realize

how much you love her. There's that moment
in an airport when you look around
and realize everyone has a soul. Everyone.

This is like those moments.
A seed, not a flower.

Everything Happening

My roses are blooming,
my yellow roses, and a child

is dying of hunger
or disease or a gunshot or grief,

and someone is laughing
and someone is crying,

and someone is lifting a cup, a star
is exploding, a heart

is breaking, the wind is blowing
over a desert, over a forest,

over the sea, and it is morning
and it is evening,

it is the first day and the last,
and every moment

somewhere the host is being
raised in the air,

in the air, in the air.

How It Holds Together

The light that shines around Jesus
they call a *mandorla*, an *almond* of light,
like the light around the moon
this morning as it sets into the trees.

One by one across the sky
the morning stars wink out.

The Lord comes walking towards me,
holding something like a hazelnut
in the palm of his hand.

This is all that is created,
he says, and it seems to me
so humble and small

I wonder how it holds
together at all.

II.

SOMETHING ELSE
I DIDN'T UNDERSTAND

Something Else I Didn't Understand

The old woman with the raggedy hair
was waiting for me at the door of the church.
I had the key. It was early, very cold.
I said no, and no again. I can't let you in.

When I came out later to look for her
she was sleeping against the wall, heaped up,
and we were told, never try to wake them.
They're confused then, uncertain, as we all are,

as in the afternoon once when I woke up
from a nap and the sun was shining through
the window. My eyes were blurry, out of focus,
and for a moment the green and yellow leaves

of the trees outside sparkled like facets
of something else I didn't understand.

Contralto

It's hard to love you, Lord, on a gray day
driving to a dirty town and entering
a dirty house smelling still of morning bacon,

with two barking dogs, one big, one small,
and a dying woman, who is enormous,
the folds of her flesh pooling out at her sides

as she leans back in her recliner, praying
the Rosary through her yellow teeth,
answering me each bead, *Holy Mary,*

Mother of God, pray for us sinners,
now and at the hour, in a voice I never
expected: a deep, silky contralto.

Doublewide

Patty and Joe's doublewide was weathered and worn,
and when I walked in it felt like home.
Joe was glad to see me, smiling through his crooked teeth.
The coffee pot sputtered on the cluttered countertop.

The night before he'd left a message on my phone,
that he was so lonesome for Patty
he thought he might *blow his friggin' brains out*.
But the thing about short-term memory loss
is that every day starts anew.

I'll never forget the day I married them,
that sweet old widow and that lonely, battered man.
Patty wore a simple print dress,
Joe a straw cowboy hat with a feather in the band.

We were standing by the tabernacle in the front
of church, and taking Patty's hand,
and looking into her eyes, Joe said, haltingly:

ain't no mountain high enough . . .
ain't no valley low enough . . .
ain't no river wide enough . . .

Joseph Canyon

In my father's house there were no pictures of my mother.
He took them down when she died, and the pictures
of my brothers, too, and of me, and hung a few of himself
instead, as a little boy, about eight or nine,
grinning at the camera. Behind him a cabin. A river.

That summer I drove into the desert. I drove and drove
until I started to cry. I was driving by a canyon, Joseph Canyon,
and the grief rumbled up from my chest
and into my shoulders and out through my throat and eyes.

It's a deep canyon, of exposed, rocky layers,
and they say Chief Joseph was born there.

In the long winter that he fled the army he guided the people
up a narrow passage further north, single file,
the warriors and the women and the children wrapped
in their woven blankets,
deeper and deeper into the falling snow.

What We Do for Ideas

The man at the hospital waved me away.
He didn't want me to pray with him.
He wasn't old but I'd never seen anyone so thin
who was still alive. No teeth.
He was hugging his knees to his chest in his pain.
Look at me, he cried, gasping,
when I asked how he was.
I was able to stand at the door and wait
because there were long pauses between gasps.
But he waved me away again
with a floppy arm, and I was glad to go.
His bitterness was terrible.
You could see his bones.
It's so sad, what we do for ideas.

Pull

When Peter reached up from his bed
I had already turned to leave,

so as he took my hand and pulled it
to his chest, I was nearly
sideways, one foot out the door.

He was wasting away,
he glowed—*cachexia* they call it—

and he looked at me from deep
within the sockets
of his eyes, pulling me back

as I pulled against him.

I don't think he was saying
goodbye.

I think he was saying:
you know the way.

Misreading Darwin

He lived not only his own life,
he lived also in the lives of others.
—*Janet Browne,* Charles Darwin

1. CHEMISTRY, THE CULTURAL APPROACH

We didn't have to do experiments, we just had to think
about them, and that's my method still. I don't like specimens.
I like shelving. Not collecting but collections.

The way Darwin said he abhorred the sea, every swell and slap,
the whole five years, but loved his tiny cabin beneath the poop deck,
with its nooks and crannies and clever drawers, though of course
he was really out there, too, scrambling over rocks
and skinning iguanas. He could do it all: geology, zoology, botany.

Back home in County Kent he spent the mornings in his study
surrounded by his books and instruments. He loved
to write on foolscap. Sometimes a sentence. Sometimes a word.

He wasn't an atheist.
He was just very, very slow. He was polite.

I am the vine and you are the branches,
as Buzz Aldrin said from the moon, though this was off-mic,
of course. He was talking about Jesus.

Then he put a host on his tongue, drank a thimble of wine,
resealed the bag, and slipped it back in a pocket
on the sleeve of his suit.

2. THE WREN IN THE IVY

Darwin wrote sitting on a chair
with a board spread across his lap.

He was always sending his children out
to collect beetles and report on the pigeons,
and he was always asking farmers
what they had seen and what they knew,
and shopkeepers, and the postman.

Anybody. He was interested.

I have a laptop, of course,
and so I often write in chairs.

Yesterday what I saw was a wren
fluttering in the ivy,
and when I went to investigate
I saw that it couldn't fly anymore.
It was injured and in hiding.

It looked right at me, blinking
the two black dots of its eyes,
and as it blinked
nothing else on its body moved.

It was otherwise still.
I think it knew me.

3. ANNIE

When I say that Darwin wasn't an atheist
I just mean he seems like such a nice man.
He was shy. He was sad. He was flatulent—
that's why he always excused himself after dinner.

He spent eight years studying barnacles, everything
about them, until he was the world's expert
on barnacles, all the different kinds,
with their hard shells and soft, creamy bodies.

He loved to walk in his garden,
admiring the trees, but only at the appointed time.
His house was the ship and his wife the captain
and he the voyager, alone with his thoughts
every day, filling page after page.

The children told time by the creak of his door—
though they were always racing in, too,
stealing a rock or a feather, and he let them,
and sometimes he talked to them or took them
in his arms and kissed them on their ears,

and when his little Annie died he so forgot himself
in a letter to a friend he called her
a little angel. An angel. He just couldn't believe
she was gone. He just wasn't thinking.

4. OUR WIVES

Darwin married his cousin, Emma,
and later came to love her dearly.

I met Barb in the band—she played the drums
and I played the clarinet—
and I loved her from the start.

After their second child died, the youngest,
a boy, Darwin bought a billiard table.
He researched it thoroughly first
and bought the best, and he liked to play
as he was thinking,
banking shots off the soft, velvet edges.

My brother and I used to play pool
down at Gazebos, in a shadowy corner
beneath a big hanging light,
the felt a brilliant, emerald green,
but I never sat at the bar until a week
after Barb and I were married.

I'd just turned twenty-one and Dad
bought me a beer
and we sat and talked. It was surreal.
It just didn't seem possible.
Everything was still on the surface.

Scythes

An old woman hired us to scythe
a vacant lot beneath a tall, white billboard.
Rusty scythes with wooden handles.
Dry weeds and dry grass and the sound

a scythe makes, and the leaping
of grasshoppers, and the sun beating down
and the cars rushing by. The dark stilts
the billboard rose on smelled of creosote.

Lunchtime she brought us sandwiches,
spam on white bread, with ketchup, wrapped
in aluminum foil, and we straightened
our backs and thank-you-ma'am-ed.

I'll never forget that sandwich.
That morning. What I can't remember
is what the billboard said.

Keeping Faith

The first moment happened right after he died
as she walked from the bedroom down the narrow hall,
praying to a God she wasn't sure she believed in
to forgive him his sins and welcome him home.
She had taken two or three steps when something
like a wind rushed by her, low to the ground,
about knee-high, whooshing towards the front door,
and it seemed to her like happiness. Like glee.
She doesn't remember where she was

when the second moment happened, but an hour
or so later she heard his voice in her head: *this is real,*
Ann. It's real. Keep faith! He was insistent,
almost angry, the way he could be, and since then
she's been wondering what exactly he meant.
Every day she walks down the street to the mailboxes,
ninety-two now, wobbly and frail, and as she walks
she says the Our Father, slowly, line by line—
she gets in about five, up and back—and every day

as she repeats the words in her head she wonders
what faith she is supposed to keep and how
she is supposed to keep it. Should she go back
to church? Should she give more away? Keep *faith*.
and sometimes the cherry trees are blossoming,
and sometimes the rain is falling. Sometimes
only flyers crowd her box. Sometimes she finds
another letter from someone who loves her.

Treasures

When they finally stripped off the tiles
and ripped out the floor, there were big gaps
between the joists and a whole system
of elbows and pipes. It'd always been there,

the water had always been running
through it, all those years as my children
grew and changed and finally left home.
I'd just never thought about it.

In the center was the drain itself, lumpy
and encrusted, misshapen with lime,
like something ancient they'd pulled up,
streaming, from the floor of the sea.

Panoramic Views

The panoramic views of the Gale Crater on Mars
make me think of Walla Walla early on a summer morning
before it gets too hot. Those lovely bare hills.
A vague blurriness in the air. Except that the hills are closer,
the horizon is closer, everything is on a smaller scale,
like in the John Day Valley, too, where the Reverend Condon
discovered the forty-four-million-year-old tiger bones.
He wasn't worried. Evolution showed the grandeur of God.
I love the way the highway rises and then dips into those little folds.
The way in the Middle Ages they believed the heavens
towered above us, level after level, but like a great building,
vertiginous but not infinite. The way the world is a stage
and we the players in it, and I am Ebenezer Scrooge and I know
all the lines and everything is about me and I love
all the characters and all the people playing the characters,
Alan and Cathy and Shane, but in relation to me,
to the story I am in and I am the star of. It's so hard to think
about anybody else. Dorothy in ICU, intubated,
casts on her arms and legs. Peter at home in his hospital bed,
looking out the window at the rhododendron
and the dogwood and the fern in Mary Lou's stepped garden,
terraced up to the top, almost vertical, like the Book
of the Gospels, split open on the ambo.

Listening to *Middlemarch* on the Way to South Dakota to Visit Our Oldest Son

Every day we drive deeper into the story.
It's afternoon, and through our windows the desert
flows by, barren and dry, but in our minds
it's morning, after light rain, *and the scent of the earth*
is sweet along the lanes and by the hedgerows—
or it's evening, and the shadows gather in the library,
and Dorthea sits sadly in a corner, holding
back her tears, *as if she must quell every impulse in her*
except the yearnings of faithfulness and compassion.

At Little Big Horn, where the Cheyenne and the Sioux
swarmed the Seventh Cavalry, we are worrying
about young Will Ladislaw, with his uncertain prospects.
At Mount Rushmore, beneath the great faces,
we are wondering about Rosamond and Mr. Garth
and the Reverend Farebrother, and all the people
in the village, with their hopes and fears and schemes.
We mortals, men and women, devour many
a disappointment between breakfast and dinnertime,
the narrator tells us, and the sentences roll on,

and the story gathers momentum, and we know
in the end everything will make sense, all will be well,
and the voice rises and falls, it pours out,
that rich, plummy voice—the voice of the narrator,
she who sees into every heart, omniscient
and wise, she who knows every urge and motive.

I have never understood my son. I've never been sure
if he is happy. I see him crouching on the prairie,
studying the communities of the mice and the bees,
the subtle tracks they make, the absences they leave,
above him an enormous sky with enormous clouds.
I see him walking down a dusty road. I see him
standing by a crumbling fence. Is he lonely? Afraid?
If we had a keen vision and feeling of all ordinary
human life, it would be like hearing the grass grow
and the squirrel's heart beat, and the fields
are flowing by, soybeans and acres of corn, miles
of corn, and it's muddy, it's flat, it's been raining,
and we should die of that roar which lies

on the other side of silence, but we are back behind
the wheel, we are going home, we have taken up
where we left off, and she is there, she hasn't left us,
she is always telling the story, her voice
steady and measured and calm, above the hum
of the tires. She knows where we are going.

Riding My Bike Through the Coast Range

When I hear the song of the white-crowned sparrow,
I think of biking with my friend through the Coast Range,
two middle-aged men on a weekend,
one day over and one day back, two fathers, two friends,
up and down the rainy backroads,
through the alder and the fir and the thick salal,

and once as we passed an open field,
chains zinging, the *deeeee da-da-dee-dee* rising up
from somewhere in the wet grass,
and how I turned and shouted, *did you hear that*?
and how he smiled and shook his head,
admiring all the things that I could name.

By the end of the day he was so far ahead
he could stop and take this: a steep valley choked
with trees, the raw, red side of a hill,
and there, on the road, so far down
you might miss it, what turns out to be me.
That white blur is my face.

Intersections

Lucy says it was God who saved her
when she veered away, and I say *yes*.

But what about all the cars that don't miss
by inches? All the intersections
we don't get through? Every moment
we feel peace or joy somewhere else

people are dying. Time slows.
They seem to be watching themselves
from a distance. It's raining or the sun
is shining and now they know this.

They think of all the other stars
and all the other galaxies
and now they know
that every star is for them.

The Door to That Room

I can't seem to remember the faces of my students.
What I remember is Achilles's shield
and Paolo and Francesca whirling around
in Canto V, which really isn't about love at all.

She's not even looking at him. Also my clean shirts
and the way they tucked into my khakis
and the sense of standing in that room at the top
of the stairs and all the bodies in it and their breathing.

I knew the man who hung the door.
He was a poet. He was in charge of all the doors.
He knew how to install
the piston and sleeve so that every day

when I walked out of that room,
the door slowly closed behind me.

The Song in the Desert

A song playing in the desert in the duplex
where we live, *Volare, oh oh, Cantare, oh oh oh,*
the grownups sitting around the kitchen table
in the dimness, and I walk in and stand before them
and begin to talk—I don't remember what I say—
but I am happy, I am joining in, and my father
reaches out and slaps me across the mouth.

Backhanded. *Let's fly way up to the clouds,*
away from the maddening crowds. We can sing
in the glow of a star that I know of . . . My father
patrols the border, he is in the Border Patrol,
studying the dust and the sand for the tracks
left by the mothers and the fathers so desperate
to come in. *Let's leave the confusion*

and all disillusion behind . . . a rainbow together
we'll find. At the hospital I kneel before his chair
and shout, *Don't be afraid! Don't be afraid!*
But he doesn't know me. He thinks I'm his brother.
At the firing range he fires, and what returns,
shivering, is in the shape of a man. *Volare,*
oh oh, Cantare, oh oh oh oh

How Slow I Am to Believe

When I brought Dorinda communion as she was dying,
I put a whole host on her parched, white tongue—
and she sat up in bed, and she sputtered

and choked. She was a wonderful woman.
In the end she was laughing, and I was laughing, too.

Today in the hospital when I asked Mary
if she wanted to receive, she said, quietly, *I don't think*
I deserve it. But she did, she is loving and kind,
and I put a whole host on her parched, white tongue—

and she sat up in bed, and sputtered and choked.
For a while she couldn't breathe.

I'm so sorry, I kept saying, as I fumbled
for the water, shaking my head
at how slow I am to believe.

Everything I Let Go Of

One of us is dead.
One of us sleeps in his van, parked
at the curb in front of his sister's house.
I've just retired.

In the morning I walk through
the summer woods
listening to the birds, amazed.
Disbelieving.

On earth when you put down a cup
it stays there, as Scott Kelly
said when he was
living on the station. But now

everything I let go of
floats away.

The Nurse and the Child

I was at the mall when the hospital called,
the old men circling in their trainers,
and the weary mothers in their sadness,
and the children, vacant stores

dark behind their grilles. The baby lay
in a bassinet among the monitors and tubes
next to her mother's bed, wrapped so
tightly you could only see her tiny,
wizened face. And the mother reached

across the railing and wept, and the father
stood beside her, and the nurse
in her scrubs, weeping, too, but the baby
never flinched when I tried

to pour a little water on her head.
It spilled from her brow and ran down
her cheeks, and the nurse came,
and knelt, and folding a paper towel,
gently wiped it away.

III.

RECOGNITION

Recognition

I was walking down a flight of stairs,
and an old woman was walking
below me, carefully, one step at a time,
arm in arm with a younger woman,
dark-haired and slim.

They were talking in low voices,
and I only saw them from behind.
I assumed the girl was leading,
helping the old woman down.

But when they reached the landing
and turned to leave, I saw
that I was wrong, as I often am.
The slim young woman was blind.

Come, Holy Spirit

It helps to look at the branches of trees
when you tire of all the actors who have played Jesus
and all the paintings, all the beards and ribcages
and knees. Look at the sky. The clouds in the sky.

But these, too, are moments. Are temporary.
Everyone has a body. The students come up
one by one, whispering what they want us
to pray for, and we put our hands on their heads

and call the Spirit down. Pray for my anger.
Pray for my grief. Pray for my loneliness,
one young woman asks. She has been crying,
and she leans in so close I feel the warmth
of her tears. A wisp of her hair.

My Dog Ate My Rosary

It wasn't malicious. He just did it, cracking
the olivewood beads like nuts,
swallowing others. He didn't eat it all.

The crucifix remains and a few
of the beads, and he didn't eat the silver chain—
the real silver chain. This was expensive.

I bought it in Rome. It was blessed by the Pope.
It was the rosary
I would be buried with, the clerk said,

in her heavily accented English,
but that's not how things are.

In the mornings now when I let Bumble out,
I find beads all over the yard.
Prayers are everywhere.

The Things of the World

It's not true that the things of the world don't know us.
The bookshelves glow when I walk into the room,
and even when I don't. The couch is right where I left it,
ready to receive me. Death is not the only way

to win an argument. I pick up the remote, and there's
Spencer Tracy in *Father of the Bride,* in black and white,
looking right at me with his big Irish face and talking
man-to-man. When he bends over to tie his shiny shoes
he sticks his tongue out of the corner of his mouth.
His house is large and white, and there are lace curtains
on the windows and curlicues on the chairbacks,
and in the high, shadowy corners a certain silvery light.

Watch for this. Whenever Tracy gives a speech,
before he starts, he sticks his hands in his pockets and looks
down. He's looking at his mark, at the cross
on the floor of the stage, and he wants us to know this.
He is exactly where he is supposed to be.

Shining Like the Sun

I don't know why I'm always starting
these arguments with Pat. No one can write
a biography of Jesus.

Jet skis shoot across the Sea of Galilee,
skimming over the waters. On the crowded slope
of the Mount of Olives, I saw a sign
for a barbershop: *A Cut Above*.

When Debbie asks me how I'm doing,
I just ramble and joke. I don't know what to say.
A hundred years from now

it won't make any difference anyway.
In ten thousand years we'll still be
shining like the sun.

The Fights

Hugo and Wright liked to watch the fights
on TV, jabbing along the way my dad did. They
were poets but they liked blood, too,
the way the heads sometimes snapped back.

Reading about this the other day
I realized I don't like this sort of thing anymore
and never did, really. I don't know why
it's taken me so long to see this. Hugo liked to tell

the story of how he and Wright once gave a ride
to a young woman after a reading.
She was trying to tell them only Jesus matters,
only Jesus, and after a while they stopped

the car and threw her out. They'd had enough
of that. I'm that woman.

What He Meant

When I drove to Spokane to see my dad
the smoke from the wildfires
was as acrid and thick as the clouds
the angry make on the third cornice of purgatory.

I couldn't see a thing until I drove away,
back down the gorge and along the river,
where the air was fresh and the leaves
were turning. *I will never forgive you,*

he said as I was leaving. He was hugging
me in the carport. I could hear
his hearing aid trilling. But I think
I know what he meant. *Forget you.*

Quitting Cross Country

When I told Coach Long I was quitting the team,
it was cool, he understood—though he said
he'd just figured out what my name would be.
He always studied the boys as they ran, their posture

and stride, the looks on their faces, then gave
each boy a metaphor. *Caveman. Scooter. Breeze.*
I've been wondering again what my name
would have been. I've been sitting

in the morning darkness, remembering
the long afternoons, how the boys would gather
around him, hopping up and down on
their rabbity legs, then bound away into the hills.

This is my name, and this is your name, too:
Beloved Son. Beloved Daughter.

All That I Have

We're in a busy shopping mall, very crowded—
this was before the virus—and an ordinary-looking man
walks out of the crowd into the center of the atrium.
He's middle-aged, wearing a leather jacket, hands in his pockets.
And he starts to sing. He opens his mouth and starts to sing,
loudly and clearly. At first you think he's crazy,
he's some kind of crank, but then you realize, wait a minute,
his voice is beautiful, it's powerful—he's singing a famous aria—
he's singing *Nessun Dorma,* from Puccini. This guy's a tenor,
this ordinary man who has emerged from the crowd
is a tenor, and he's a great tenor, and his voice is building
and rising, and people are stopping and looking, the expressions
on their faces are changing, people who would never be
caught dead at an opera, who don't have any idea what opera is,
they're stopped in their tracks. One little girl turns around
and looks up at her mother, amazement in her eyes.
O look at the stars, the tenor sings, *that tremble of love*
and hope, and his voice gathers and swells, it rises to its climax,
and he hits that final, high note, and he holds it, holds it
until it's ringing in the air of that crowded mall,
and something transcendent has happened, something
wonderful has risen out of that ordinary gray day, something
excellent and pure, and everyone knows it, they feel it,
and they burst into applause, burst into tears. They whistle
and call. And the tenor smiles, and looks around,
puts his hands in his pockets, and walks back into the crowd.
He disappears. O that I might hold my one note
and walk away! O that I might disappear!

Mr. Moody

Is it really true that Mr. Moody marched
in John Phillip Sousa's band? Sousa died in 1932.

This was 1966 or so. I was twelve.
I'd take the bus downtown and climb the stairs
and sit in a room that smelled of natural gas.

Mr. Moody always sat on the chair beside me
as I played him what I'd practiced.
He was old then, very old, thin and bald,

with thick, knobby fingers, and when he stuck
the clarinet between his rubbery lips
and began to blow, the air escaped through

the holes where his mouth didn't close.
The Liberty Bell. The Yellow Rose.
The crowds cheering and the flags waving.

The Stars and Stripes Forever,
row after row after row.

The Spiritual Life Compared to Two Toys

It's as if every morning you shake
a Magic 8 Ball and words float up
in a window on the bottom,
white letters against black plastic:

Without a doubt or *Signs point to yes*

Except most days no words float up,
and when they do,
you have to wait and see.
What persists?

You bobble and tilt until you get
the bb's into the holes on the face
of a clown, the eyes, the nose,
the wide, red mouth—

a bump, and they're all
rolling around again.

The Elements

If we could send a drone back through time
to hover over the empty tomb the way it hovers now
over the Newman Center barbeque, a small drone
with four propellers, taking b-roll for the website,
it would still just see the tops of heads:

St. John's, St. Peter's, St. Mary Magdalene's.
The top of the gardener's wide-brimmed hat.
It's hard to see the face of Jesus.

One night at the old Newman house before
they tore it down, as we sat on those old thrift store
couches and talked about the gospel,
I glanced into the kitchen and saw a mouse pop up
on the stove top. Then another, and another.

They'd crawl up through the coils of a burner,
look around, then quick, back down, like soldiers
in the trenches. It was the funniest thing.

All night long they kept popping up
in the elements.

Where This Is Going

A man with a handlebar mustache leans
over his wife's wheelchair, adjusting the armrests
and smoothing out her pale print blouse.
He must dress her every morning. Lift her in.

Her head is canted to one side. She seems to be able
to move only her right hand and forearm.
Peace, I say, at the Sign of Peace, and she smiles
her sideways smile, looking up with her eyes.

A Holocaust victim goes to heaven and tells God
a Holocaust joke. *That's not funny*,
God says. *I guess you had to be there*, the man says,
and God smiles and gently shakes his head.

He knew, of course, where this
was going.

The Chase

By the time I walked into the backyard Bumble
had already raced down the ravine and up the other side
and was streaking after a deer on the ridge, right to left—
I could see him—then across the road and into
the further woods, and so I hurried after him, running
along a grassy ledge through the trees and around

the edge of a small pond I hadn't known was there,
until finally I saw them, not six inches apart, the deer
and the dog, lunging at each other and taking turns
trying to bump each other with their heads, Bumble wild
and barking, the doe leaning against a tree, sick,
it seemed to me, or starving, too exhausted to run.

A friend says I shouldn't clench my fists when I tell
this story, I shouldn't be afraid—she wants me to be happy
and at peace all the time—but when I grabbed for Bumble
and the doe skittered away, brushing against my arm as it
jumped, and Bumble bounded after her, whirling, knocking me
backwards onto the soft, forgiving ground, and the doe
dove into the pond and started swimming, breasting the thick

green layer of algae, and Bumble leapt in after her,
paddling furiously and bumping against her with his shoulder,
and the doe bumping against his with hers, the two of them
veering in circles in the water, left, then right, until Bumble
started to struggle, until he seemed to panic, looking up
at me with wide, frightened eyes, drenched and bedraggled,

trying, frantically, to make for shore, and reaching it
finally, and trying to scrabble up the muddy bank, and falling
back, again and again, and me lifting and pulling him
by his collar, his fur, trying to heave him up and out, trying
not to tumble in myself, trying not to get pulled under—
I wasn't roaring anymore. I was trembling. I was holding him

in my arms. Gasping. Soaked with mud. The both of us.
Where the doe went I don't know, whether she managed
to clamber out of the pond and slip away into the trees again,
or even if she drowned, in her weakness and her panic. I've
worried about her since. But I wasn't panicked anymore
and I wasn't afraid. I was amazed. At how close we'd all been.

Holding Up Father Matt

Father Matt's hands shook so hard it took him
forever to eat his noodles. By the time
he got a forkful to his mouth, half had wobbled
off the tines and he'd have to start again.
But he didn't seem to mind, and in the end
we had a good lunch. We became friends.

One morning at Mass he started to tip over
backwards. He couldn't keep his balance.
So I reached out and pressed my hand against
the small of his back as he blessed the bread
and wine: *may your Spirit come upon these gifts,*
he prayed, *that they may become for us*
the body and blood of our Lord Jesus Christ.
That way we could both remain standing.

When Barb Brings Shy to Sunrise

When Barb brings Shy to Sunrise to read
with the kids, it's like she's bringing communion.
They open their books, and Shy lies on his side,
and they reach out to stroke his scruffy, black fur.

It's not about words. Shy has a body, part
terrier, part Chihuahua, with snapping brown eyes
and little orange feet. He weighs nine pounds
six ounces. This is what people don't understand

about faith. Last Sunday at Mass, a woman
I know was a Eucharistic Minister, and as she stood
at the foot of the altar with a small ciborium
full of hosts, waiting for people to come forward,
as she stood there holding the Body of Christ,

her arms began to shake, it felt so heavy—
like the dead weight,
she told me, *of a sleeping child.*

The Deacon Comes to Dinner

The little girls run up and throw their arms
around my waist. They are six
and eight, their hair brushed and shining.

While we're waiting for dinner, they run
and get all their stuffed animals
to show me, especially a pink and yellow

unicorn bigger than they are.
They're so excited. Even years from now
they might remember me, and I know

I don't deserve this. It's not about me.
They've cut out paper crosses
to show how much they believe.

Axle Seal

The other day when I brought my car in for an oil change
they found I needed a new seal on the right front axle.
But when I picked it up and drove it for a while
the brakes were soft and there was this humming,

like I was driving on studded tires. So I brought it back,
and they checked it out again, and they said, well,
now you need a new wheel bearing, on the right side,
and that's going to cost you, hundreds of dollars.

I thought this was odd—I hadn't had this problem before—
but I don't know much about cars, so I said, OK.
Go ahead. But here's the thing. The woman who was
helping me at the desk, who could have let this go—

I was ready to pay, I wouldn't have known—this woman
went back to the mechanics and asked around
and found out it was their fault, that in replacing the seal
they'd set the brakes wrong and that this had caused

the bearing to fray. Or something. All I know
is that she called me later, and said that she was sorry,
and that they'd fix it for free. I was just grateful,
and surprised. I have no idea how any of this works.

On the Feast of Our Lady

It's really a miracle, her former jailer says,
sitting across from us in the gym
on the Feast of Our Lady of Guadalupe.

For weeks the voices had been coming from billboards
and newspapers and over the radio
in the car as she drove the kids to soccer practice,
until one day in the kitchen cutting bagels

she lifted up the bread knife and stabbed her mother
in the chest, there, in front of her children,
above the cream cheese and the peanut butter. Killed her.
A kind, white-haired woman who had come to help.

Then the red lights flashing down our street,
the yellow tape sealing off their driveway.

You don't want to know, her husband said.
You don't want to know.

Now it's years later and she is home
from the state hospital and we are all together in the gym,
my friend and her husband and her former jailer,
the whole parish is gathered, on the Feast of Our Lady
of Guadalupe, and we're eating spaghetti and telling stories,
behind us the image of Our Lady projected on a screen.

She is brown and she is bursting, she is with child,
and the light is raying out of her like fire.

A boy in a cape shuffles on stage and kneels before the screen,
our Juan Diego, the man who may or may not have seen
the Virgin one night five hundred years ago,
on a hilltop in Mexico. Who may or may not have existed.

Listen, my son, my little one, says a voice
over the PA system. *Where are you going?*

Kids running up and down the aisles.
The gym cold and cavernous, smelling of tomato sauce.
Her hair gone white now,
and she is smaller somehow, fragile,

she is sitting beside me in purple fleece,
chatting with her former jailer—*no, they won't let me drive yet*—
a quiet man with a kind face, munching a cookie,
and whatever miracle this is,
it is ordinary. No one is denying anything.

Am I worthy of you, Juan Diego asks. *Am I only dreaming?*

No, we hear over the PA. *Be certain, my son,*
that I am the Mother of the God of Great Truth.

Why I Like Prayer

Because there's not a lot to do.
I just sit and look out the window.

Sometimes I light a candle.
Sometimes I fall among thorns.

Sometimes there's a spring of living water
within me, welling up unto Eternal Life.

I feel the weight of my body.
I feel the weight of the world.

I remember Montana and playing
in the snow and that blur
beside me is Taco, our dog.

I am smiling and my brothers
are with me and we love our mother
so much. So very much.

Beautiful River

When I was young, I had an old '56 Chevy.
It was the first car I ever owned.
They only wanted three hundred bucks for it,
but Dad checked it out and it always ran great.
I could take you right now to the exact spot
along the river where the sheriff found
that car the morning after someone stole it,
abandoned, halfway down the bank,
and the river would be still flowing.
The beautiful, the beautiful river.

What is Going On

A hundred years ago the smiling man
in the wheelchair wore the same gown
his great-grandson is wearing now.

It is made of white cotton, softened
and yellowed with age, and goes
all the way past the baby's toes.

The family has been telling stories,
but quiets now and gathers around.
The mother holds the baby in her arms.

The old man is smiling, and his eyes
are clear and aware. He knows
what is going on, and for a moment
I do, too, and I stand at the font
and cup the water in my hand.

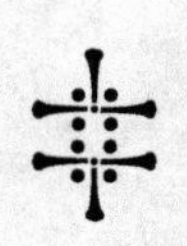

ACKNOWLEDGMENTS

I owe a great debt of gratitude to Mark S. Burrows, the poetry editor at Wildhouse Publications, for his encouragement, support, and editorial eye, and to Wildhouse for its vision and spirit. I am grateful to Molly Silverstein and Melody Stanford Martin of the press, for their friendliness and expertise.

Thank you to Richard Thorn for his generosity in letting us use his beautiful painting, "Down Misty Vale," for the cover of this book.

I am greatly indebted to Eric Dickey, Kelley Dupuis, Eric Hill, Michael Malan, and Richard Wakefield for their generous and insightful readings of earlier drafts of this book—and to Lex Runciman, for his encouragement and his insight into many of the individual poems that appear here. Thank you to Catherine Otto for her expert proofreading.

My wife, Barb, has always been my first and most important reader, and with these poems, too, she has challenged and encouraged me daily, with both patience and an unerring sense of what rings true.

My thanks to the journals that published the following poems, some of them in different forms and under different titles:

Alba: "Contralto," "Driving at Night," "Treasures," "What He Meant"

American Writers Review: "The Nurse and the Child"

Amethyst: "Everything Happening," "Something Else I Didn't Understand"

The Coachella Review: "On the Feast of Our Lady," "The Solar System"

Fathoms: "What Happens at Mass," "Relinquishment," "Love Calls Us Here"

Fireweed: "Geese"

Hole in the Head Review: "The Fights," "Waiting in the Garden"

The MacGuffin: "Listening to *Middlemarch* on the Way to South Dakota to Visit Our Oldest Son"

Notre Dame Review: "The Things of the World"

Pilgrimage: "At the Dog Show," "The Song in the Desert"

Psaltery and Lyre: "Wild Iris"

Rattle: "Misreading Darwin," "All That I Have"

Salamander: "Everything I Let Go of"

Spiritus: "Surprised"

Turtle Island: "The Pilot Whale"

Windhover: "Shining Like the Sun," "Where This Is Going"

NOTES

"To Believe is to Remember"

The title is a paraphrase of a sentence in Pope Francis's *The Joy of the Gospel:* "the believer is essentially one who remembers."

"The Solar System"

The story about the regatta in space is Arthur C. Clarke's "Sunjammer," published in 1964.

"The Trinity"

Another Beauty is the title of a memoir by the Polish poet Adam Zagajewski.

"The Scientist at the Party"

The allegory of the sphere is from Richard Taylor as paraphrased in David Bentley Hart's *The Experience of God: Being, Consciousness, and Bliss*. The arguments I make in the poem are from Hart.

"What Happens at Mass"

"We think he's the gardener" alludes to the scene in John 20.11–18, when Mary Magdalene encounters Jesus after the Resurrection.

"The Anointing"

In "the Anointing of the Sick," the one who is ill is anointed by a priest with a special oil. The "sacristy" is the room in a church where the vestments are kept.

"Relinquishment"

The quotes are from a sermon of St. Augustine included in the *Liturgy of Hours*. It's the second reading in the Office of Readings for the Third Sunday of Advent.

"Don't Be Surprised"

During the eucharistic consecration, the priest raises up the host and the cup before the congregation.

"How It Holds Together"

The image of the hazelnut is from *Showings* by the late-medieval visionary, Julian of Norwich (born in 1342, died sometime after 1416); it is found in Ch. 5 of the so-called "Long Text."

"Doublewide"

The "tabernacle" contains the consecrated hosts left over after Mass.

"Chemistry, the Cultural Approach"

"I am the vine, you are the branches" is John 15.5. Buzz Aldrin was the Lunar Module Pilot on Apollo 11, the first moon landing. He read this verse as a part of a brief communion service immediately after the Eagle landed. See Andrew Chaikin's *Man on the Moon: The Voyages of the Apollo Astronauts*.

"Panoramic Views"

Thomas Condon was a Congregational minister and geologist who discovered fossilized mammal bones in Eastern Oregon in what is now called the John Day Fossil Beds. He died in 1907. The "ambo" is the pulpit in the church where the Gospel is read and the homily preached.

"The Door to that Room"

Achilles's shield is described in Book XVIII of *The Iliad*. Paolo and Francesca are the lovers in Canto V of Dante's *Inferno*, the Circle of the Lustful.

"The Song in the Desert"

"Volare" is an Italian song recorded and released by Dean Martin in 1958 and Bobby Rydell in 1960. "Volare" means "to fly"; "cantare" means "to sing."

"Everything I Let Go Of"

The allusion is to Scott Kelly's autobiography, *Endurance: A Year in Space*.

"Shining Like the Sun"

"No one can write a biography of Jesus" is a paraphrase of Romano Guardini in *The Lord*. The last line is a paraphrase of a verse of "Amazing Grace."

"The Fights"

Richard Hugo and James Wright.

"What He Meant"

See Dante's *Purgatorio*, Canto XVI.

"The Elements"

The "crown of the gardener's wide-brimmed hat" refers again to John (20.11–18), when Mary sees Jesus but thinks he's the gardener. In a painting of this scene, "The Risen Christ Appearing to Mary Magdalene," Rembrandt depicts the gardener as a man wearing an odd, wide-brimmed hat.

"When Barb Brings Shy to Sunrise"

A "ciborium" is a bowl or other vessel that holds the consecrated hosts that are distributed during Mass. A "Eucharistic Minister" is someone who helps distribute communion.

"Beautiful River"

The phrase "the beautiful, the beautiful river" is from the American spiritual "Shall We Gather at the River?"

Chris Anderson is a Catholic deacon, poet, and retired professor of English living in Corvallis, Oregon. He grew up in Spokane, Washington, went to college at Gonzaga University, and attended graduate school at the University of Washington. After receiving a Ph.D. in English in 1983, he taught literature and writing for 38 years, 34 of them at Oregon State University. He retired in 2020.

In 1997 he completed a Masters in Theology at Mount Angel Seminary and was ordained a deacon. Since then, he has served at St. Mary's in Corvallis, as well as leading retreats and offering spiritual direction. He has written, co-written, or edited 14 previous books, including three books of creative nonfiction and three books of poetry. In 2016 Eerdman's published a book drawn from his homilies and poems, *Light When It Comes: Trusting Joy, Facing Darkness, and Seeing God in Everything*.

He and his wife, Barb, a retired pastoral associate, have lived for many years on the edge of the forest north of Corvallis. They have three children, four grandchildren, and two dogs.

For more, visit www.deaconchrisanderson.com

This book is set in Optima typeface, developed by the German type-designer and calligrapher Hermann Zapf. Its inspiration came during Zapf's first trip to Italy in 1950. While in Florence he visited the cemetery of the Basilica di Santa Croce and was immediately taken by the design of the lettering found on the old tombstones there. He quickly sketched an early draft of the design on a 1000 lira banknote, and after returning to Frankfurt devoted himself to its development. It was first released as Optima by the D. Stempel AG foundry in 1958 and shortly thereafter by Mergenthaler in the United States. Inspired by classical Roman inscriptions and distinguished by its flared terminals, this typeface is prized for its curves and straights which vary minutely in thickness, providing a graceful and clear impression to the eye.

Printed in the USA
CPSIA information can be obtained
at www.ICGtesting.com
LVHW040926091224
798490LV00009B/854

* 9 7 8 1 9 6 1 7 4 1 1 1 9 *

The divine meets us in the real world and nowhere else, Anderson suggests in these poems, coming without fanfare and often startling us with its presence. When and where should we look for these encounters? Here and now. In our ordinary lives. In those everyday moments, now and then, when something suddenly stirs within us, a reality we can't quite put into words. The quiet poems of this collection, through their clarity and craft, invite us to enter this mystery, offering us glimpses of a beauty we never expected, a wordless radiance rising in the dark. In Anderson's poetry, hope takes shape in the ordinary; wisdom lingers between the lines. In each of the poems collected here, Anderson helps us taste the mystery hidden in our lives and invites us to trust it—to dare joy and risk hope in these difficult times.

"One by one, the poems in *Love Calls Us Here* gift us with something small and bright. Nothing fancy, nothing explained, belabored, nothing but an episode of what I have to call grace. There is no other word. Just enough." — Kim Stafford, author of *As the Sky Begins to Change*

"In each poem we are led to a moment of awareness: God meets us here. They are deeply reassuring. They are also whimsical and poignant and surprising, sometimes breathtakingly apt." — Marilyn McIntyre, author of *Word by Word: A Daily Spiritual Practice*

"These plainspoken, profound, surprising, earnest poems mark Chris Anderson as one of my favorite voices in this tangled world." — Paul J. Willis, author of *Somewhere to Follow*

"Awakens readers to realize we are immersed in a world of wondrous gifts, gifts delivered through loved ones and strangers, through dogs, gardens, geese, the solar system, etc. These poems are quiet celebrations and lessons for life." — Abbot Jeremy Driscoll, O.S.B., Mount Angel Abbey, author of *A Monk's Alphabet*

Chris Anderson is a Catholic deacon, poet, and retired professor of English living in Corvallis, Oregon. He is the author of *Light When It Comes: Trusting Joy, Facing Darkness, and Seeing God in Everything.*

BOSTON, MASSACHUSETTS
WILDHOUSEPUBLISHING.COM/WIPO

Cover Photo: Down in Misty Vale by artist Richard Thorn',
courtesy of Haddon Galleries Torquay

ISBN 9781961741119
91999 >
9 781961 741119